THE
PADMAS

FIFTY STORIES OF
PERSEVERANCE

NEHA J HIRANANDANI

ILLUSTRATIONS BY DAVID YAMBEM

PUFFIN BOOKS

An imprint of Penguin Random House

PUFFIN BOOKS

Puffin Books is an imprint of the Penguin Random House group of companies
whose addresses can be found at global.penguinrandomhouse.com

Published by Penguin Random House India Pvt. Ltd
4th Floor, Capital Tower 1, MG Road,
Gurugram 122 002, Haryana, India

Penguin
Random House
India

First published in Puffin Books by Penguin Random House India 2024

Text copyright © Neha J Hiranandani 2024
Illustrations copyright © David Yambem 2024

ISBN 9780143463955

Book design and layout by Samar Bansal
Typeset in Livvic by Manipal Technologies Limited, Manipal
Printed at Paras Offset Pvt. Ltd., Kundli (Haryana)

www.penguin.co.in

To my father, with all my love

CONTENTS

INTRODUCTION

When I sat down to write this book, I tried to think back to my first memory of the Padma awards. I must have been eight or nine years old. It was a sunny March day in Delhi. I was sitting with my father as we watched a broadcast of the president conferring that year's Padma awards. Decades have passed, but what my father said that afternoon hasn't left me: 'These aren't just awards. They are a celebration.'

Thereafter, every Republic Day, when the list of Padma awardees was released, my mind wandered back to my father's words. I wondered what he meant. What do the Padma awards celebrate? The answer became clear as I understood the history of the awards and learnt the awardees' stories.

The Padma awards were instituted in 1954. Given in three categories: Padma Vibhushan (for exceptional and distinguished service), Padma Bhushan (for distinguished service of higher order) and Padma Shri (for distinguished service), the awards recognize the achievements of people from different walks of life and diverse spheres—from art and music to science and medicine as well as literature, sports and more. The Padmas not only celebrate achievement, but also service and love for the nation. And so, as they celebrate our beloved India, the Padma awards become more than a medallion. They become a feeling. They become the expression of a grateful nation as we celebrate the stories of our heroes.

Writing this book took me back to that sunny day in Delhi when I sat alongside my father. In the seventieth year of these awards, I hope reading these stories will take you somewhere special, too.

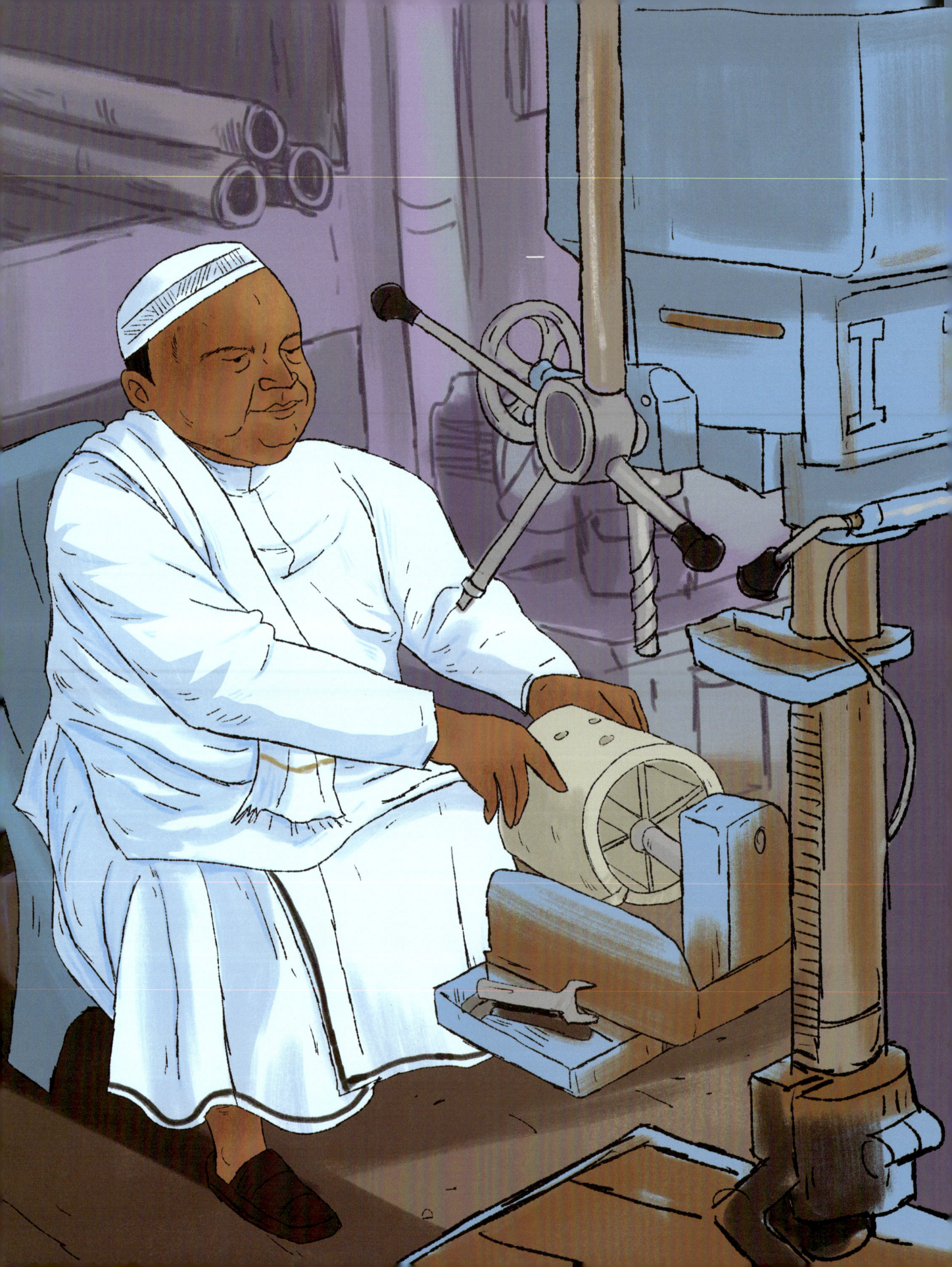

ABDUL KHADER NADAKATTIN

PADMA
SHRI
2022

INGENIOUS INVENTOR

1953-PRESENT

Meet Abdul—a clever and inventive man from Karnataka. Abdul was not a morning person and would usually sleep until late. Though he wanted to be an early riser, no alarm had the power to wake him. Then, one morning, tired of oversleeping, Abdul decided to do something about it. He found an old alarm clock and a water bottle and combined them into something extraordinary! He tied a string from the key of the alarm clock to the water bottle. When the alarm rang, the key unwound, and the water bottle tipped over, splashing water all over his face! It became his personal water alarm clock, and no one could sleep through that refreshing wake-up call.

Abdul had very little money to his name, but he had the heart of an inventor. Since he was from a family of farmers, he wanted to help others like him. So, Abdul started a workshop where he produced the most fascinating tools. He created a machine that could sharpen a ploughing blade with just a few twists and turns. Abdul then made a drill that could plant seeds and fertilize them at the same time. He also created a special boiler that could heat water for twenty people and keep it warm for a whole day.

Do you know what made Abdul famous? His love for tamarinds! He was so passionate about these tiny, tangy fruits that he created amazing devices to help farm them. One of his machines could separate tamarind seeds, and the other could slice them in a jiffy. The villagers named him 'Tamarind Maniac' because of these inventions.

So far, Abdul has invented over forty tools to help hardworking farmers. And to think all this came from a man who once loved to sleep until late!

ANNAPURNA DEVI

MYSTERIOUS MUSICIAN

1927–2018

When Annapurna was growing up in Madhya Pradesh, many people believed girls couldn't be great musicians. Her father, Allauddin Khan, was a famous musician, but he was against teaching Annapurna music. The trouble was that Annapurna simply couldn't stay away! When her father taught her brother music, she would observe them secretly and learn.

One day, when his father wasn't home, Annapurna's brother was practising his music lesson. Her brother was doing it wrong. To show him the right way, Annapurna sang the piece and did it perfectly. Little did she know that her father had returned and had been watching her all along! Annapurna was terrified, but Allauddin recognized his daughter's talent and realized his mistake.

Allauddin began to teach Annapurna the sitar, but he soon sensed that his daughter needed an even greater challenge. So, he offered her a choice between the sitar and the surbahar, a heavy and challenging instrument. Very few people played the surbahar, and certainly not women! Annapurna was surprised, but she was up for the challenge! And so her journey with music began. Annapurna began to play at concerts where she mesmerized the audience with her soul-stirring melodies. But Annapurna discovered that her heart soared only when she played for herself and taught her students.

Lost in her music, Annapurna became a mysterious recluse, spending her days with only the pigeons on her balcony. People wanted to honour her talent with awards, but Annapurna refused to leave her home. She didn't even go to collect the prestigious Padma Bhushan!

Annapurna continued to practise every day, but no one was allowed to hear her music, not even through recordings. Whenever someone requested her to play, she would say, 'I don't know how to play at all,' with a twinkle in her eyes.

PADMA
BHUSHAN
1981

PADMA
VIBHUSHAN
1990

A.P.J. ABDUL KALAM

PEOPLE'S PRESIDENT

1931–2015

Many years ago, a young boy named Abdul lived in the seaside town of Rameswaram. Once, when he was ten years old, Abdul was sitting in a classroom feeling totally confused. His science teacher was trying to explain how birds could fly. Abdul confessed to his teacher that he couldn't understand a word.

Abdul's teacher was not one to give up easily. That evening, the teacher took the entire class to the seashore, where they saw seagulls flying gracefully in the sky above. Patiently, the teacher again explained how birds flew as he pointed out their flapping wings, twisting tails and ability to change direction. He told the students that a bird's engine was powered by its own life. That moment marked the beginning of a dream for Abdul. Inspired by the seagulls, he became obsessed with the idea of flight.

With his heart set on this ambitious dream, Abdul left Rameswaram to study science at a school that was in another city. The boy who was once utterly confused in science class would become a scientist who tested aeroplanes and built hovercrafts. Abdul's passion led him to space research and, eventually, to the United States of America. He worked at the NASA space agency in the USA.

Upon returning to India, Abdul continued to reach for the stars. He helped launch India's first rocket, worked on satellite launch vehicles and championed the development of Indian missiles. In 2002, Abdul became the eleventh president of the nation. He was fondly known as the 'People's President'. Just like those birds he saw on the shimmering shores of Rameswaram, Abdul had soared and engineered his own life.

ARUNA ASAF ALI

- - - - - - - - - - - - - - - - - -

FEARLESS LEADER

1909–1996

PADMA VIBHUSHAN 1992

At a time when India was under the rule of the British Empire, a fiery young woman named Aruna Asaf Ali yearned to free her beloved motherland from foreign rule.

In 1942, Mahatma Gandhi gave a powerful speech that changed the course of India's history. He boldly called upon the British to leave India. Mahatma Gandhi planned to hoist the forbidden Indian flag at Gowalia Tank in Mumbai. Hoisting the flag would mark the start of the Quit India Movement. Somehow, news of this plan reached the ears of the British authorities. They quickly arrested Mahatma Gandhi, Jawaharlal Nehru and other key leaders. With all the leaders in jail, it seemed like the flag-hoisting would not happen.

The crowds had already gathered at Gowalia Tank and were eagerly waiting for the flag to be unfurled. But who would do it? That was when young Aruna decided to take action. She was standing amidst hundreds of British soldiers and knew that her actions could lead to her arrest. In an extraordinary display of courage, Aruna dashed towards the flagpole! With the crowds and the soldiers watching, she tugged at the flag's rope. After a few determined pulls, the Tricolour unfurled gracefully. As the flag fluttered free, the crowd erupted into cheers! At that moment, brave Aruna had challenged the might of the entire British Empire. Aruna became a heroine, a symbol of courage and determination.

Following India's independence, Aruna became the first mayor of Delhi. She was awarded the Padma Vibhushan and the prestigious Bharat Ratna, India's highest civilian award, in recognition of her unwavering dedication to her country.

ARUNIMA SINHA

UNSTOPPABLE ATHLETE
1989–PRESENT

Arunima loved many things, but most of all, she loved playing volleyball. Once, when she was travelling by train for a volleyball event, a gang of thieves cornered her. They wanted her gold chain. Arunima tried to fight them but was pushed off the moving train. She landed on the railway tracks and was hit by an oncoming train. Arunima lay on the tracks all night—alone, terrified and in great pain.

In the morning, she was taken to a hospital. As she was lying on the hospital bed, the doctor came in with terrible news. To save Arunima's life, one of her legs had to be amputated. Arunima knew she could never play in the national volleyball team again. Most people would have lost their minds with this terrible news. But Arunima decided to set herself an unthinkable challenge—to climb Mt Everest!

Once she had made up her mind, Arunima was unstoppable. Even though her body was still healing, her spirit was already climbing new heights. She started her training as soon as she left the hospital. Other mountaineers couldn't believe what they were hearing—was Arunima really planning to climb Mt Everest with one artificial leg and a rod in the other?

The climb was challenging for Anrunima. Her artificial leg would slip on the icy mountain slope, and the strain made her legs bleed. 'Many times, the prosthetic leg just came off on the mountain, and I fell,' Arunima said later. But she kept going. 'The mind holds tremendous sway over the body. Once I had decided that this is what I would do, I let nothing get the better of me.'

Within two years of losing her leg, Arunima had climbed the tallest peak in the world and planted the Indian flag in the snow! Since then, Arunima has climbed the seven highest peaks on all seven continents.

PADMA SHRI 1971

PADMA VIBHUSHAN 1986

BABA AMTE

PILLAR OF COMPASSION

1914–2008

Murlidhar Devidas Amte was different from the others in his wealthy neighbourhood. His family lovingly nicknamed him Baba and, as a child, he had all the toys one could dream of. He also had something special inside him—a kind heart and a keen eye for justice.

As a young man, Baba followed his parents' wishes, got married and began working as a lawyer. However, he soon decided to take matters into his own hands. Baba wanted to make the world a better place—a place where everyone could have a fair and happy life. He started waking up at 3 a.m. every day, well before sunrise. He joined ragpickers to collect waste and clean the town's dirty gutters. By working alongside the ragpickers and cleaners, he wanted to show that everyone deserved respect. Then, one day, something happened that shook Baba to the core.

Baba met a man named Tulshiram who was sick with a disease called leprosy. With holes in place of a nose and without fingers or toes, Tulshiram's body was difficult for anyone to look at. Even Baba felt scared when he saw Tulshiram. But he decided he was going to beat his fear and help Tulshiram. His parents were outraged at his actions and cut off all contact with him. But Baba did not let this upset him. Instead, he gathered his wife and children, a cow, a dog and six people affected by leprosy and went to live on a barren piece of land. There, they built a special place called Anandwan where people with leprosy could live in peace.

Baba went on to receive many awards because of his incredible work. He believed that the most useful person was someone who helped others when they needed it the most. Looking at Baba's life, it is clear that being a hero doesn't mean you need a cape. Sometimes, all you need is a heart full of love.

BERTHA GYNDYKES DKHAR

TRAILBLAZING TEACHER
1959–PRESENT

In the lush hills of Shillong lives Bertha who faced an extraordinary challenge growing up. Bertha was born with a rare disease that was slowly taking away her vision. She knew that soon she would not be able to see anything. Failing eyesight meant getting a job was difficult, so Bertha started selling jams and pickles to sustain herself.

Things changed when Bertha became a teacher at a school for children with disabilities. That's where she discovered Braille, a special system of reading designed to help the visually impaired. Braille books have raised dots that the blind can touch with their fingers and read the books; they use their sense of touch instead of their eyes to read.

While at the school, Bertha began to learn Braille so that she could teach it to her students. But then, inspiration struck! Bertha realized her students would find it easier if they could learn Braille in Khasi, their mother tongue, instead of English. Determined to make it happen, Bertha started doing research. Her hard work paid off as she successfully invented a Braille system that allowed blind children to access education in their beloved Khasi language. When she introduced her invention at the school, joy and wonder filled the room!

News of Bertha's achievement spread, and her invention became a beacon of hope for many. She printed Braille textbooks and conducted workshops to share her knowledge. Today, the Braille system in Khasi stands as a testament to Bertha's ingenuity. Although she lost her eyesight, Bertha changed the lives of countless children. Each time their fingers touched those little dots, their mother tongue came alive.

BIRUBALA RABHA

TRUTH HUNTER
1954–PRESENT

In a remote village in Assam, a brave woman named Birubala Rabha lived. The people in her village believed in witches and other scary superstitions. Whenever something went wrong, they thought it was a witch's work. The villagers would always label some poor woman as a witch and blame her for the problem.

Like others in her village, Birubala grew up believing these stories. One day, when her son fell ill, Birubala rushed him to a local doctor who told her that her son was cursed and would die in a few days. But the boy continued to live. It turned out that her son had typhoid and recovered after medical treatment. This made Birubala realize that the stories about witches were false.

Once, there was a big meeting in her village to discuss the witch problem. Birubala couldn't keep quiet any longer. She stood up and boldly declared, 'There are no witches; witchcraft does not exist!' The crowd roared with anger. Hundreds of people surrounded her house, demanding that she sign a document saying she was lying, but Birubala refused.

In the years that followed, Birubala faced many challenges. Angry mobs threatened her with sticks and tried to throw her out of the village. But Birubala stood her ground and kept going. She travelled to nearby villages and helped women who were accused of practising witchcraft. She would march into police stations bravely and demand justice for the women who were victims of witch hunts.

In the end, Birubala's bravery paid off. In 2018, a new law was passed in Assam that finally banned witch-hunting. What a victory!

Often, we know when something is wrong, but we don't risk speaking up for what's right. Birubala did this not once, but again and again.

PADMA SHRI 1990

CHANDRA PRABHA AITWAL

QUEEN OF THE MOUNTAIN

1941–PRESENT

In the majestic land of Uttarakhand, where snow-capped peaks reach for the skies and the air echoes with tales of bravery, lived a young girl named Chandra Prabha. She didn't like being confined to a classroom and preferred to spend her time hiking, where her adventurous spirit could run free. With every mountain she climbed, her passion grew stronger. Soon, Chandra Prabha longed for the ultimate challenge—to climb the formidable Nanda Devi, the second-highest peak in India. As per legend, the goddess Nanda Devi watches over the mountain and blesses those who respect her land.

Chandra Prabha joined an expedition to climb the magnificent peak. It was a tough trek, and when she was midway, Chandra Prabha fell ill. She had an upset stomach that ached, and pus oozed from one of her ears. Discouraged, she turned back to base camp while her team continued upwards. 'The expedition was over for me at this point,' she said later.

Then, the goddess of the mountain smiled upon Chandra Prabha! A doctor from another expedition prepared a magic potion for her to sip while climbing. With the potion in her pocket and determination in her eyes, Chandra Prabha set off the following day to climb the mountain alone. Her progress was slow, but she didn't waver. She borrowed equipment, making do with whatever was available, and continued to sip the potion.

As the sun set, Chandra Prabha reached the camp of her teammates and surprised them; they never expected to see her there. Night had fallen, but she pressed on in the dark, determined to reach the summit. With each step, the climber's spirit soared. And then . . . it happened! Chandra Prabha conquered the mighty Nanda Devi mountain! With snow under her feet and a carpet of stars overhead, she felt triumph like never before. It was as if she had glimpsed the goddess herself.

PADMA SHRI 2016

DEEPIKA KUMARI

BULLSEYE QUEEN
1994–PRESENT

Deepika lived in a small town in Ranchi, Jharkhand. Her father was a rickshaw driver, and her mother was a nurse. With such a modest income, Deepika and her family lived in a small hut. Their home didn't have any comforts—no fans, tables or a bathroom. Their only piece of furniture was a single bed that the whole family shared.

There were days when the family couldn't even afford a square meal, let alone fruits. Interestingly, fruits played an important role in Deepika's life. There were several mango trees in Deepika's neighbourhood. When she was younger, Deepika would bring down the fruits by hitting them with stones during mango season. Later, she fashioned a bow and a few arrows out of bamboo to get to those delicious fruits. Though Deepika enjoyed such carefree moments, she remained worried. She knew that her family needed money. So, to help her parents financially, Deepika decided to take up archery. After all, she had practice with mangoes!

Archery required being physically strong, but Deepika was thin and frail. Many people doubted if she could do it. 'Tumse toh bhari dhanush hai, yeh sab nahin hoga tumse!' (You can't do this; even the bow is heavier than you!) said the owner of the archery academy that Deepika wanted to join. Undeterred, she convinced the owner to give her three months to prove her skill. Deepika gave it her all in those few months. She would be the first to reach practice in the morning and, sometimes, would stay up all night, practising her posture in front of a mirror. Often, she would practise twice as much as the coach instructed.

Soon, Deepika began to hit every bullseye and rose to the number one position in archery in the world! So far, she has won at the Commonwealth Games, the Asian Archery Championships, the World Archery Championships and the World Cup.

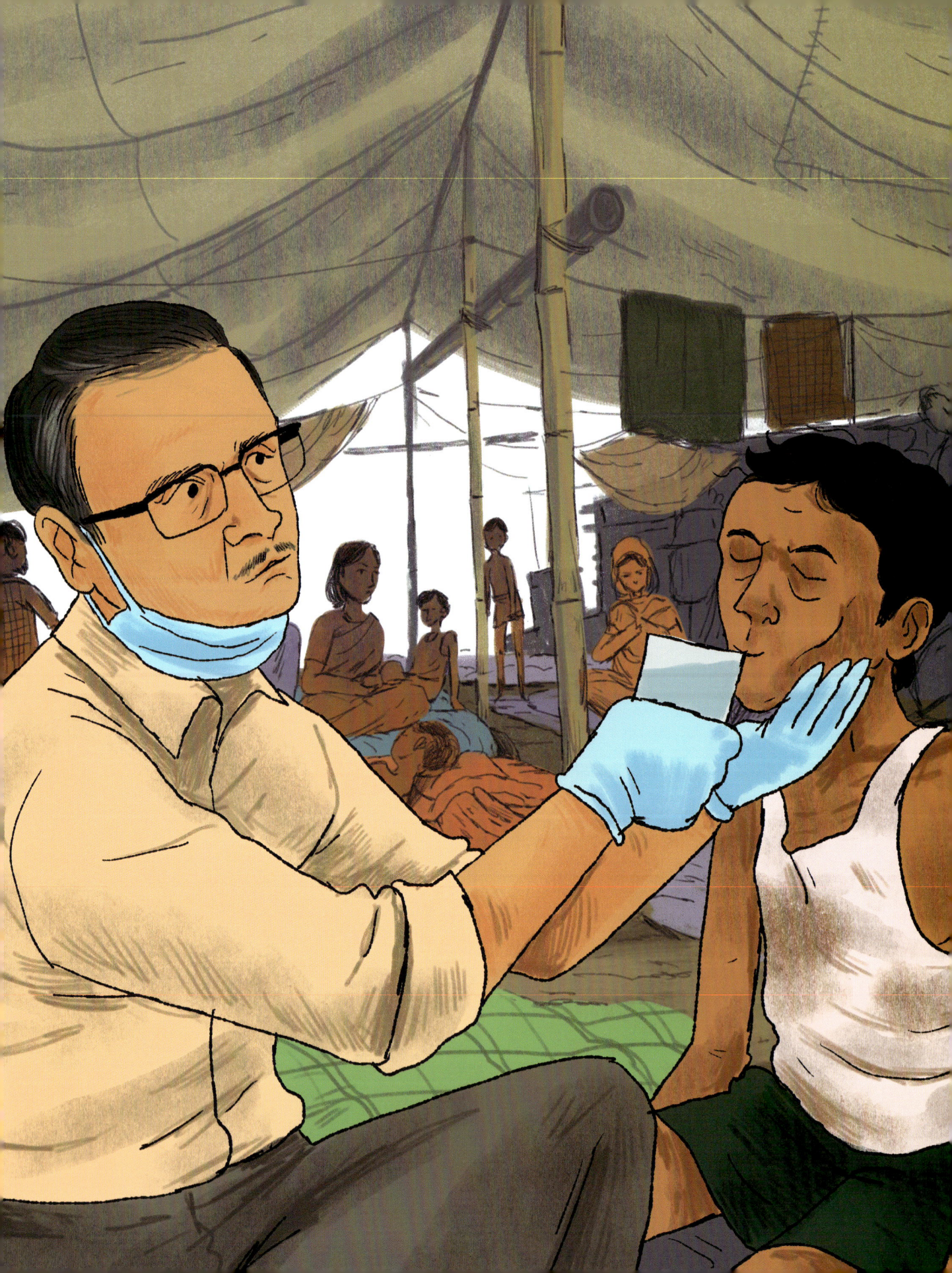

DR DILIP MAHALANABIS

- -

DOCTOR WITH A DREAM

1934–2022

In 1971, there was a war in Bangladesh, and millions of people fled to India for safety. They lived in temporary settlements called refugee camps. At that time, a doctor named Dilip in Calcutta was trying to come up with a treatment for dehydration. When we fall ill, the body gets dehydrated and needs water and minerals. Dr Dilip was looking for a way to provide a balanced mixture of water and minerals to a patient orally. He came up with a simple oral rehydration solution (ORS).

One day, Dr Dilip was sent to a refugee camp where thousands of people from Bangladesh were living in unhygienic conditions. It was monsoon season, and rain, mud and mosquitoes were everywhere. The people were getting sick, and thousands had already died due to dehydration caused by the disease cholera.

Dr Dilip did not know what to do. Only two people in his team knew how to give medicines using needles. Besides, the camp was not clean enough to use this method of treatment. So, Dr Dilip decided to try something new. He made the refugees sip ORS—the solution he had developed. Some doctors protested, saying Dr Dilip should wait for permission from the authorities before giving ORS to the sick. But people were dying, and Dr Dilip knew he couldn't wait.

The ORS was easy to administer. The patient just had to drink the solution. Miraculously, most of the patients recovered from cholera!

If Dr Dilip had waited for official permission to use ORS, many more lives might have been lost. Even after his strategy had worked, people couldn't believe that lives could be saved by something so simple. Today, the whole world knows the value of ORS, which has been hailed as the greatest discovery of the twentieth century.

DR KUSHAL KONWAR SARMA

- -

ELEPHANT DOCTOR
1961-PRESENT

PADMA SHRI 2020

Kushal lived in Assam, a state that is home to many elephants. One day, Kushal's grandmother adopted an elephant named Lakshmi. Although his parents discouraged Kushal from spending time with Lakshmi, he would sneak out of his house and meet her. A friendship developed between the boy and the elephant. Together, they spent hours roaming orchards, eating fruit and chasing butterflies. But this extraordinary time didn't last long. Kushal's family had to move to another town, and he was separated from his beloved Lakshmi.

After two years, at the age of eight, Kushal returned to his village. He longed to see Lakshmi again but was faced with sad news instead. Lakshmi had suffered a severe injury and lost her life because there was no doctor available to treat her. Kushal was overcome with grief. He vowed to become a veterinarian, a doctor who cares for animals. The young boy worked hard to achieve this goal, and soon, Kushal became Dr Sarma.

Today, Dr Sarma has cared for over 10,000 elephants, including wild and rogue elephants. Despite the danger, Dr Sarma loves every moment of it. One time, he spent an entire night in a tree trying to sedate a wild elephant. He performed surgery on an elephant that had been shot five times. Once, he even captured a rogue elephant that was charging at him! For Dr Sarma, his work is pure joy. He once said, 'I am happiest when I am near elephants . . . Even at this moment, if you tell me an elephant is trapped or in need of help, I will pack my bags and drive to that location.'

On weekends, when most people take a break, Dr Sarma continues to work. India's Elephant Doctor has never taken a weekend off and takes care of over 700 elephants a year!

DR MAMBALLAIKALATHIL SARADA MENON

HEALER WITH A HEART

1923-2021

In the late 1940s, Dr Menon had almost completed her medical degree, but something inside her called her to a special mission. She was curious about the human mind. She wanted to understand how it worked—how it processed feelings and emotions, and, most importantly, how to help it when it wasn't behaving as it should.

In her final year, Dr Menon attended a class on mental diseases at the Government Mental Hospital in Chennai. What she saw made her heart ache. The mentally-ill patients looked different—their hair was messy, and their clothes were dirty. They seemed lost in their own world and were talking to themselves. What made Dr Menon sadder was that nobody seemed to be taking care of them.

Dr Menon's heart went out to a sixteen-year-old girl she met there. The girl was confined to her bed, crying and shouting. The doctors could only give her medicine to help her sleep, but they didn't have a solution to help her overcome her struggles. Back in those days, not many people understood problems related to the mind, and sometimes they thought that people who were feeling sad were just being lazy.

Not one to turn away from a challenge, Dr Menon was determined to make a difference in the lives of these neglected individuals. She trained to become India's first female psychiatrist and worked towards changing how doctors approached mental illness. Through her work and teachings, she ensured that doctors wouldn't ignore patients like that young girl ever again. She stopped people from dismissing and shaming those who were mentally ill.

Dr Menon founded an NGO called SCARF to help heal the mentally ill and support their families. Throughout her remarkable career, she earned numerous awards, but the most rewarding part for her was witnessing the transformation of the people she helped.

DR RATAN CHANDRA KAR

FRIEND OF THE JARAWA

1954–PRESENT

The Andaman and Nicobar Islands are a group of more than 800 islands surrounded by shimmering water with beautiful fish. These islands are also home to ancient tribes, such as the Jarawa, who, until recently, did not have contact with the outside world. The Jarawa cherished their isolated life and would not allow outsiders—not even doctors or the police—to enter their territory.

Then, one day, trouble struck—there was a terrible outbreak of measles on the islands. The disease was killing the Jarawa, but there was no medical care available. The tribe was on the brink of extinction. That's when Dr Ratan Chandra Kar, a government doctor, was asked to step in.

Dr Kar was nervous about the tribespeople. Armed with poison-tipped arrows, Jarawas were known to be violent towards outsiders. 'Will they accept me, or will they attack me?' wondered Dr Kar. Even though he was afraid, Dr Kar persevered because the tribe urgently needed help. Carrying coconuts and bananas as gifts, Dr Kar reached the Islands. He went to see his first patient, who had hurt himself in a hunting accident. As Dr Kar approached the patient's hut, the tribespeople followed him, eyeing him suspiciously. He cleaned the patient's wound and applied medicine. When Dr Kar returned the next day, his patient had improved. Slowly, the tribespeople began to trust Dr Kar and allowed him to give them medical care. Dr Kar started learning the Jawara language and soon became fluent in it. Over time, he evolved from being a doctor to a treasured friend of the Jarawa.

Thanks to Dr Kar, the measles outbreak was controlled, and the Jarawa tribe was saved from extinction. Without him, this unique tribe would have been lost forever. And so, in the heart of these paradise islands, a heart-warming story of friendship unfolded.

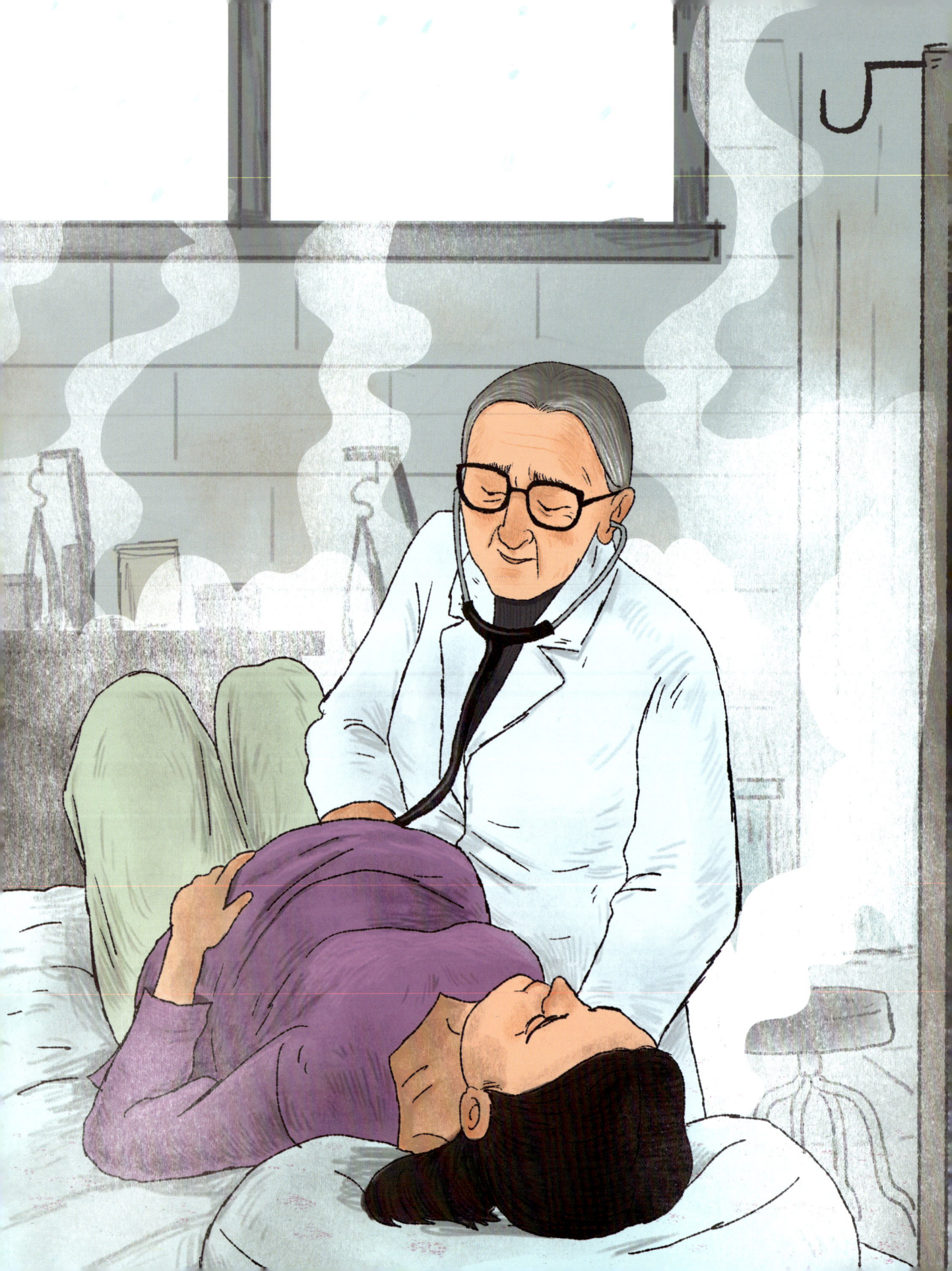

DR TSERING LANDOL

PASSIONATE DOCTOR
1945–PRESENT

Tsering, also known as Dr Landol, lives in Ladakh, a beautiful but remote part of India known for its extremely cold weather and snowy mountains. Tsering is Ladakh's first gynaecologist, a doctor who focuses on women's health. She has delivered babies and responded to emergencies even in temperatures of minus twenty degrees Celsius!

When Tsering grew up in Ladakh, there weren't many hospitals or clinics around. Then, one day, she met a doctor at a school function and was inspired to become one herself. She felt doctors, with their stethoscopes around their necks, always looked impressive. Young Tsering worked hard, studied medicine and became Dr Landol.

Dr Landol started working at the local hospital, but all was not hunky dory. The hospital had no heating system, and the temperature indoors was biting cold all the time. Sometimes, women who came to deliver their babies and their newborns died because of the freezing cold. The hospital tried to solve the problem by using traditional coal heaters. But these heaters added dangerous gases to the rooms, making them unsafe for women and babies. That's when Dr Landol had a simple but superb lifesaving idea! She suggested that the hospital use the Kashmiri *hamam* system, which utilizes a wood-burning stove, to keep the labour room warm. It was a simple idea that didn't require a lot of money, and luckily, the hospital approved it. The temperature in the labour room rose, and then the best thing happened! Almost all the babies who were born in the hospital survived, and more women started coming to the hospital for the safe delivery of their babies!

Even after her retirement, Dr Landol continues helping people through medicine and her revolutionary ideas.

DURGABAI DESHMUKH

REBEL REFORMER

1909–1981

PADMA VIBHUSHAN 1975

In a land where bravery blooms like wildflowers, there lived a girl named Durgabai. She was born in Rajahmundry, Andhra Pradesh. Right from the beginning, Durgabai had a sparkle in her eyes that said, I'm going to do things my way!

As per the custom in those days, Durgabai was married by the time she was eight. But no one could make this outspoken rebel do something she didn't want, and what she wanted was to study. So, she simply refused to go to her husband's house, determined to focus on her studies.

Soon after, Durgabai started attending a school where the lessons were taught in English. She was furious that the British were forcing children to learn English. With fire in her eyes, thirteen-year-old Durgabai walked out and decided to start her own Hindi-medium school! She had recently learned Hindi and wanted other girls to learn it, too. At her new school, girls would not be forced to study English.

Durgabai's bold spirit followed her wherever she went. At fourteen, she volunteered at an event that several important leaders were attending. No one was allowed inside without a ticket. Then, the most influential man in India, Jawaharlal Nehru, walked in. But he did not have a ticket. Durgabai recognized him, but she stubbornly refused him entry. No ticket, no entry! Pandit Nehru was amazed by the young girl's determination.

Durgabai's heart was as big as her dreams. She worked tirelessly to help girls, setting up organizations to train them for jobs. Soon, she was invited to join the country's most prominent organizations, such as the Constituent Assembly and the Planning Commission.

For all her work, Durgabai was awarded the Padma Vibhushan. The little girl who thought, 'I won't go to school if it's not fair!' ended up doing amazing things. Sometimes, a little bit of rebellion goes a long way!

E.K. JANAKI AMMAL

EMPRESS OF FLORA

1897–1984

PADMA SHRI 1977

Janaki grew up in Kerala, surrounded by dense forests and vibrant valleys. As a child, she loved playing in her father's enchanting garden, where flowers swayed in the breeze and magnificent trees reached for the sky. Janaki loved to explore the wonders of nature, and the garden helped her do so right in her backyard!

As Janaki grew older, she saw her sisters get married. But Janaki's dreams were different. She was determined to become a scientist, something unheard of for women in those days. Eventually, Janaki won a scholarship to study in the USA. There, she studied botany, the science of plants. Eight years and much hard work later, Janaki became Dr Janaki Ammal—the first woman botanist in India.

During World War Two, Janaki was working in England. Those were dark, dangerous times, and bombs dropped from the sky without warning. But not even bombs and bullets could stop Janaki's passion for plants. When the bombings happened, Janaki would hide under the table or sleep under her bed to stay safe. Once the skies cleared, she would return to work, cleaning the broken glass from the shelves as if nothing had happened. 'Life isn't worth it without a sense of danger,' said the ever-optimistic Janaki.

During her career, Janaki achieved many incredible things. She bred a new variety of Indian sugar cane to make it sweeter. India no longer had to import sugar cane from Indonesia! So whenever you enjoy a glass of sweet sugar cane juice in India, remember to thank Janaki. Every spring, a white magnolia blooms in the Royal Horticultural Society's garden in the UK in Janaki's honour. 'My work is what will survive,' said Janaki, and that beautiful magnolia reminds us that it has.

ELA BHATT

VOCAL VISIONARY

1933–2022

In the bustling city of Ahmedabad, there lived a woman named Ela Bhatt. When she became the head of the women's wing of the Textile Labour Association (TLA) in the city, Ela saw something that upset her greatly—many women workers were struggling to make ends meet. These women did odd jobs like weaving, cleaning and selling vegetables. Even though they worked hard, they were paid just a few rupees, and their families were starving. Ela wanted to help these women. So, she created a group called SEWA (Self-Employed Women's Association) to teach working women their rights and help them learn new skills.

Ela faced many challenges at first. Her idea was new and nobody who could help liked it. In fact, Ela could not even get SEWA registered as a trade union in the beginning! There were other hurdles, too. They needed money so that the women could work independently. But the banks refused to give them a loan. Not one to be deterred, Ela found the solution to this problem. She started the SEWA Cooperative Bank. Again, she faced opposition. Even her own family discouraged her, saying the poor women would not repay loans. But Ela decided to trust these hardworking women. And it paid off!

Slowly, under Ela's leadership, the women started working together and running their own small businesses. SEWA grew bigger. More women joined, and they helped each other. Ela made sure SEWA was a team, and just a few years after it was set up, SEWA had over 7,000 members!

SEWA has gone from being a small group to an organization with millions of women! Today, it is the single-largest trade union in India. When Ela first launched SEWA, she had a great deal to lose. Everyone had said that helping these women was impossible, but Ela showed us what can happen when we take a chance on people.

PADMA
SHRI
1962

GOSTHA BEHARI PAL

- - - - - - - - - - - - - - - -

BAREFOOT HERO
1896–1976

In the world of football (or soccer, as some call it), there was an incredible player named Pal. He played every single game without shoes! While his opponents had fancy football shoes that gave them an advantage on the muddy field, Pal liked to play barefoot. But shoes or no shoes, Pal soon earned the nickname Great Wall of China because his opponents felt they just couldn't get the ball past him. Playing against Pal felt like playing against a wall!

In 1936, Pal and his team were playing a match against an all-English team in Kolkata. The referee made decisions based on the players' skin colour instead of how they played. Pal knew this was wrong and decided to stand up against this unfairness. He told his teammates to lie down on the ground during the match. All the players lay on the ground in silent protest, as if to say, 'We won't play until things are fair.' In a peaceful way, the players showed they wanted things to change. The match authorities wanted to punish Pal and his team, but Pal walked off the field before they could do anything.

Pal retired after this incredible match. He had made a huge impact, even though he never played football again. Pal once said, 'In an era when we (Indians) were humiliated and insulted in every step of life . . . the football arena was the only one place where we could fight . . .'

People loved Pal so much that they made a life-size statue of him, named a road after him and even issued a special stamp. Even though he never wore shoes while playing, he left behind giant shoes for other Indian footballers to fill. Gostha Behari Pal was truly a hero, both on and off the field.

HAREKALA HAJABBA

ORANGE SELLER
1952–PRESENT

On a sunny day in a tiny village in Karnataka, something happened that turned an orange seller into a changemaker. Hajabba sold oranges at the local bus depot, a job he had done for years, earning about INR 150 a day. Life carried on in this manner. Then, one day, something changed.

'It was a Saturday,' remembers Hajabba. That day, a foreigner came to his stall and asked the price of the oranges. 'How much?' asked the foreigner in English. Hajabba was stumped! He had never studied in school and could speak and understand only Kannada. He so wished he could understand and reply to the foreigner. At that moment, Hajabba realized the importance of schooling.

'An idea struck me to start a primary school . . .' said Hajabba. Like many other villages, his village, Newpadpu, didn't have a school. The children there grew up without an education. Though Hajabba wanted to open a school, many villagers did not support him. But he was determined to change things and started a small primary school in a local madrasa with a few students. Soon, the number of students increased. Hajabba needed a bigger space and a proper school building. He decided to use his life's savings and buy a piece of land. On that land, he built a bigger school building that would accommodate everyone.

At first, Hajaba had to manage the school all by himself. This included cleaning the place and boiling drinking water for the children. Soon, news of the work he was doing spread. People from Newpadpu and beyond started to send whatever money they could to help Hajabba run the school.

Today, Newpadpu's first school proudly educates the village children till class ten. The orange seller who opened a school now has a new dream—to open a college!

H.M. SEERVAI

HONOURABLE ADVOCATE

1906–1996

In the bustling city of Mumbai, there lived a man named Hormasji 'Homi' Maneckji Seervai. Homi lost his father when he was a young boy, and his mother became his mentor and advisor. Despite his modest beginnings, Homi had a thirst for knowledge and a strong sense of justice that led him to achieve remarkable things.

Homi studied hard and chose to become a lawyer. He was a fearless advocate and did well as a lawyer. But what made him really stand out was his understanding of the Constitution. The Constitution of India is the most important law book in the country; think of it as a rulebook that guides Indians on how to live and work together. No one knew the Constitution like Homi did. He wrote several books that analyzed this important book. Homi came to be known as the 'bulldog of the Indian Constitution' because of how fiercely he protected it.

Homi did not hesitate when speaking his mind, and honesty became his hallmark. Once, a lawyer asked him for advice on a case. Homi spent a lot of time researching and reading many books to find a solution. He even held conferences to discuss the case. When Homi finally gave his advice and quoted his fee, the lawyer who had asked for his advice was surprised—the fee was much less than what they had expected! The lawyer urged Homi to quote a higher rate. Homi refused and said that he had been asked for advice on the assumption that he knew the law. So, there was no need to adjust the fee. Later, someone else asked Homi why it was wrong to charge high fees, especially when clients were willing to pay. Without a moment's hesitation, Homi said, 'If a man was willing to be robbed, would you be a thief?'

HOMI JEHANGIR BHABHA

PHENOMENAL PHYSICIST
1909–1966

PADMA
BHUSHAN
1954

Homi was born into affluence and was well connected to the Tatas—one of India's most influential families at that time. But Homi had a problem. While his family wanted him to become an engineer and join the Tata company, Homi's heart danced to a different tune—the enchanting melody of physics! Homi was captivated by the mysteries of the universe and wanted to unravel its secrets. However, upon his father's insistence, he went to study engineering in England.

Homi tried, but he couldn't find joy in engineering. In a letter to his father, he compared his desire to study physics to that of great musicians like Beethoven who didn't listen to anyone but followed their passion. 'It is no use saying to Beethoven, "You must be a scientist, for it is a great thing," when he did not care two hoots for science. I, therefore, earnestly implore you to let me do physics,' he said. Finally, his parents agreed! Homi promised them he would achieve great things in the field of physics.

It so happened that Homi was on vacation in India when World War Two broke out in Europe. Seeing this, Homi decided to stay back in India and help his country in any way he could. While atomic bombs had been used to harm people, Homi realized that atomic energy could also be used to help India. With the backing of the Indian government and the help of the Tata family, Homi started working on India's atomic programme. He established institutes such as the Bhabha Atomic Research Centre and paved the way for India to become a nuclear power. Under his direction, India even made an atomic bomb in record time. When convincing his father to let him study physics, Homi had said, 'Physics is my line. I know I shall do great things here'. And he was right. Think of Homi if you ever have to convince your parents to let you follow your passion!

INDRA NOOYI

CORPORATE CONSCIENCE
1955–PRESENT

If there was one thing that Indra's family believed in, it was hard work. Indra's mother wanted her to score top marks in school, and her father encouraged her by saying that there was no limit to what she could achieve if she tried. And try, she did! She worked hard throughout college and even after graduation. Then, in 2006, she became the Chief Executive Officer of PepsiCo, Inc., a global food and beverage company. Indra was now the head of one of the biggest companies in the world!

PepsiCo produced several products, including fizzy drinks like Pepsi and snacks like Kurkure and Cheetos. Unfortunately, not many of these were healthy. Indra called these products 'Fun for You' as she knew they were tasty. But she also knew that many people would prefer healthier snacks and drinks.

Indra decided it was time for a change, and she urged PepsiCo to make healthier products. The company soon introduced two new product categories: 'Better for You' and 'Good for You'. These snacks were not only yummy but also much better for the body as they had less sugar, salt and processed ingredients. Snacks like baked chips as well as drinks like fruit juice started being produced under the PepsiCo brand. Now, making big changes often leads to big problems, and not everyone at PepsiCo was happy about the change. The company had been doing so well for so long. Many in the company didn't see the need to change anything. But Indra's mind was made up. She was determined to promote a healthier lifestyle for her customers.

Indra's instinct turned out to be spot on—people everywhere loved the new healthy products! With Indra leading the way, PepsiCo became an even bigger company. To the delight of parents everywhere, Indra showed us that taste and health can go hand in hand!

ISMAT CHUGHTAI

- -

FREE-SPIRITED WRITER

1915-1991

PADMA SHRI 1976

Many years ago, in Uttar Pradesh, there lived a girl named Ismat. She and her family were Muslims, and they followed the religion of Islam. Back then, many believed that people of different religions shouldn't be friends with each other or even share food! One of Ismat's closest friends was a Hindu girl called Sushi. Even though people said the two shouldn't be friends, Ismat and Sushi didn't care. When they would find ripe guavas, the girls would take bites from the same fruit, showing everyone that friendship was mightier than strict customs. They were rebels!

One day, Ismat went over to play at Sushi's house. It happened to be Janmashtami, the birthday of Lord Krishna. Ismat held an idol of Krishna that belonged to her friend. Sushi's family was shocked. They immediately snatched the idol from Ismat and sent her out of the house. Even Ismat's family was taken aback, as idols are not part of the Islamic faith. But Ismat believed that all people and religions were equal. Years later, when Ismat and Sushi reunited, they continued to brush aside those old rules. They laughed and shared bites from the same ladoo.

Being a rebel isn't easy, especially when you have to stand up against your family. In those days, many girls were not allowed to go to school. Ismat, too, had to fight with her family for her education. Eventually, Ismat went on to write many powerful stories, many of them about friendship. She became a celebrated writer, even though she was awful at spellings.

PADMA
BHUSHAN
1955

PADMA
VIBHUSHAN
1987

KAMALADEVI CHATTOPADHYAY

FEARLESS CRUSADER

1903–1988

When Kamaladevi was a little girl, child marriages were common in India. Young Kamaladevi was married at eleven, widowed at twelve and remarried at sixteen! Despite her circumstances, Kamaladevi remained an independent thinker. She always stood up for what was right, no matter where she was.

In 1941, Kamaladevi was travelling on a train in the United States of America. At that time, America practised unfair segregation. They didn't allow people of different skin colours to sit together in public places, like trains. Kamaladevi didn't want to follow this rule, and she sat in a compartment with a sign that read: 'Whites Only'. Kamaladevi decided she wouldn't let an unfair rule decide where she could sit.

A stern-looking ticket collector came by and ordered Kamaladevi to move. When she asked the collector why, he replied, 'This is the rule, and you better obey it or you will regret it.' Still, Kamaladevi didn't leave the compartment. The ticket collector walked away angrily but returned soon. 'Which land do you come from?' he asked her this time. Now, Kamaladevi could have proudly explained that she was a distinguished visitor from India. Her bravery had convinced Mahatma Gandhi to include women in the Indian freedom struggle. In fact, she was such an important part of the independence movement that just a few months before, she had had tea with the American president to discuss women's rights. But she did not tell the ticket collector any of this. Instead, she replied, 'It makes no difference. I'm a coloured woman . . . and I have no intention of moving from here.'

Kamaladevi didn't budge from her seat, and the ticket collector realized he had lost the fight. As the train chugged along, it carried Kamaladevi's courage and spread the message that all colours are beautiful and every person deserves respect.

KESHAVA SHANKAR PILLAI

PADMA SHRI 1956

PADMA BHUSHAN 1966

PADMA VIBHUSHAN 1976

MASTER CARTOONIST

1902-1989

When Shankar was a young boy, he came across a funny sight—his teacher had fallen asleep during class! The sight of the sleeping teacher inspired Shankar, and he quickly sketched a cartoon. As you can imagine, the headmaster wasn't happy with the cartoon (nor was the teacher!) and Shankar got into trouble. But despite the headmaster's annoyance, one of Shankar's uncles recognized his talent and encouraged him to keep drawing. And he did!

As an adult, Shankar continued to draw cartoons fearlessly, poking fun at important people, even viceroys and prime ministers! Shankar's humour spared no one, no matter how powerful. His cartoons began to be published in *Hindustan Times*, and soon, people from all over the world came to know and love his work. His cartoons became so popular that one day Mahatma Gandhi asked Shankar, 'Did *Hindustan Times* make you famous, or did you make *Hindustan Times* famous?' Even though Shankar made fun of politicians, he had a friendly relationship with many of them, and he encouraged them to laugh at themselves. Jawaharlal Nehru once said to him, 'Don't spare me, Shankar!' The cartoonist took this seriously, poking fun at Nehru in over 4,000 cartoons!

Ever the child with his cartoons and comics, Shankar was convinced that children were much more interesting than adults. He wrote and illustrated several children's books. 'Children are beautiful, unspoilt, lovable. They deserve the best of everything,' he said. So, Shankar established the Children's Book Trust and the Doll Museum. Both of these wonderful places still exist in Delhi's Bahadur Shah Zafar Marg. You can head there to be inspired by Shankar who taught us to be brave, creative and fearless about sharing our talents with the world.

MAJOR RALENGNAO 'BOB' KHATHING

PIONEER OF PEACE

1912–1990

PADMA SHRI 1957

Major Ralengnao Khathing believed in the power of words over weapons to solve even the trickiest of problems, unlike most soldiers. Better known as 'Bob', Major Ralengnao served as a soldier in the Indian army at an important time. Even though India had achieved Independence, the country's border areas faced constant threats. One such problem area was the beautiful region of Tawang, which is in Arunachal Pradesh today but was earlier under the then independent Tibetan government.

Aware of Major Ralengnao's talent for solving conflicts amicably, the Indian government called upon him to convince the people of Tawang to join India. So, along with a team of 200 soldiers, Major Bob set out on an epic journey to Tawang. The group trekked up rugged mountains, crossed deep valleys and faced several obstacles along the way. When they finally reached Tawang, Major Ralengnao knew that he had to win the hearts of the locals. He called for a meeting with the village elders and other important people at a magnificent monastery.

In the peaceful surroundings of the monastery, the locals told the major about the challenges they faced under the Tibetan administration—how they paid heavy taxes and were oppressed. With kind words, Major Ralengnao began to weave his magic like a wizard casting a spell. He spoke about Indian democracy and promised that India would treat Tawang with respect. And then something incredible happened! Without firing a single gunshot, Major Bob had convinced the people. They joyfully accepted the Indian flag he had brought, and with cheers of happiness, Tawang willingly became a part of India.

What a historical moment it was! A celebration of the power of words over weapons, all thanks to the soldier who turned battles into conversations and enemies into friends!

"My aim is to win the Olympic gold"

MARY KOM

PADMA SHRI 2006 · PADMA BHUSHAN 2013 · PADMA VIBHUSHAN 2020

MIGHTY CHAMPION
1982–PRESENT

ary lived in a village in Manipur. She loved sports, but her family didn't have the means to support her dreams.

When she was a young girl, Mary heard the story of Dingko Singh. Dingko was a Manipuri who had risen from humble beginnings to become a boxing champion. His story inspired Mary, and she secretly approached a boxing coach in Imphal to train her. But when the coach saw Mary, he laughed and said, 'You are a girl; boxing is not for you.' Mary pleaded with the coach to give her a chance, and eventually, the coach relented. From that moment, Mary dedicated herself to boxing. She tirelessly trained every day. Even though she was slender, she didn't let her size stop her from practising boxing. Often, she would spar with her own reflection in the mirror, determined to become a champion.

All this time, Mary's parents didn't know she had taken up boxing. Her secret remained a secret until the day Mary became the state boxing champion, and her picture was printed in the newspaper. Mary's father saw his daughter's photo and ordered her to come back from Imphal. Mary did return home, but with a shining gold medal! From then on, Mary was unstoppable. She went on to become a six-time world boxing champion and an Olympic bronze medalist. After that day, her father beamed with pride when he found his daughter's photo in newspapers from all over the country.

Despite being one of the lightest championship boxers, Mary is one of the mightiest. 'When I started boxing, people laughed at me and said, "What can women do in boxing?"' she said once in an interview. But Mary has proved that no dream is too big for any person, no matter how small they may be.

PADMA
SHRI
1972

MARY VERGHESE

DOCTOR WITH WINGS
1925–1986

Mary was a little girl with a big dream—she wanted to become a doctor. But almost a hundred years ago, it wasn't easy for girls to purse such careers. Mary's parents wanted her to be a teacher, but she wanted to help people through medicine. Seeing her determination, her parents supported her. After several years in medical school, Mary's dream came true—she was finally a doctor! Unfortunately, life was about to become harder.

Just after her graduation, Mary was on her way to a picnic. But this picnic day changed Mary's life forever. The car she was travelling in met with a terrible accident, and Mary was left paralyzed from the waist down. The girl who dreamt of healing others was herself going to be in a wheelchair forever. But Mary was not one to give up easily.

Soon enough, Mary learnt how to take care of herself and manage without her legs. She could even drape a sari on her own. But she was worried. What about her dream to help others? That's when Mary met another doctor who had a brilliant idea. He suggested that she could perform surgeries while sitting in her wheelchair. You might know that doctors always stand over patients during surgeries. So, a 'sitting surgery' was a crazy idea! It had never been done before, but Mary was excited to try.

In no time, Mary was successfully performing complicated surgeries sitting in her wheelchair. To make an even bigger difference, Mary started a special centre for people with disabilities. She wanted to help others like her who faced challenges but had big dreams, too. Mary worked hard, and even though she couldn't walk, she felt like she could fly! 'I asked for feet,' said Mary, 'and I have been given wings.'

Mary—India's first paralyzed surgeon—received the Padma Shri in 1972. Of course, she rolled up to receive the award in her trusty wheelchair.

MELVILLE DE MELLOW

- - - - - - - - - - - - - -

GUIDING VOICE

1913–1989

PADMA
SHRI
1963

Long ago, when the radio used to be the main source of entertainment and information, there lived a man named Melville de Mellow. Melville was a radio broadcaster whose voice was warm and sweet like honey; it comforted anyone who heard it. Before television and other gadgets, families would gather around radios to listen to voices like Melville's that brought them peace and joy.

Whenever an important event happened in the country, Melville would report the incident live for his listeners. For many years, Melville remained the reliable voice that India turned to for both good and bad news. On the terrible day that Mahatma Gandhi died, Melville spoke on the radio for over seven hours! Though his tone was serious, his speech was emotional. Melville's voice was like a gentle hand that held people's hearts during tough times. During that gloomy period, Melville gave people hope, saying that Gandhi's memory was like a lamp that would shine forever.

Melville was very dedicated to his work. Once, a friend told Melville that he had heard a pack of jackals howling on his way home. Years later, the broadcaster remembered this and asked his friend to record the jackals so that he could use the sound for a radio documentary. His friend did not want to take the trouble of making a recording and sent Melville a recording of British foxes instead. But Melville was an expert at recognizing sounds. He scolded his friend and said, 'I want the Indian jackal, not the British fox.' His friend had no choice but to go out at midnight and wait to make a recording.

The legacy of Melville's comforting voice has continued to inspire generations of radio broadcasters and storytellers. It is because of Melville that many young people dream of sharing their voices with the rest of the world.

PADMA SHRI 1966

PADMA BHUSHAN 1973

PADMA VIBHUSHAN 1991

M.F. HUSSAIN

MAVERICK ARTIST

1915–2011

Picture a man with a beard as white as snow, walking around barefoot, carrying a paintbrush as long as three long rulers put together. That was Maqbool Fida Hussain, one of the most famous artists in the world. Sometimes, he waved his paintbrush like a conductor leading a symphony, and other times he used it like a walking stick!

Maqbool's paintings were as vibrant as him—horses and women in splashes of red, yellow and blue—and simply unforgettable. Where many painters took months or years to finish a single painting, Maqbool often finished a painting in a single sitting. Sometimes, he didn't stop at one; he would make several paintings without even getting up!

Once, he arrived in Europe just a day before a major exhibition of his work. But there was a problem—there weren't enough paintings to exhibit! So, straight from the airport, Maqbool went to the nearest shop that sold art materials. After that, he locked himself in his hotel room and got down on the floor, spreading his canvases before him. All night long, the artist painted. By the next morning, Maqbool had made enough paintings to fill the entire exhibition.

Maqbool was once asked how he managed to make so many paintings. He replied, 'I get up at five or six, and I always feel it's my first day. I don't get bored with sunrise. I then work hard for three or four hours.'

And after that?

'Ah, the rest of the time,' he said, 'I think it is very important just to loiter around.'

PADMA SHRI 1959

PADMA BHUSHAN 1967

MIHIR SEN

- - - - - - - - - - -

SWIMMING AGAINST THE TIDE

1930–1997

In a village in Odisha, a boy named Mihir entered the world too early and too small. Though his beginning had been tough, little Mihir was full of big dreams. Mihir's family was of humble means. His father was the local doctor, and his mother sold eggs and milk to bring in extra money. Mihir studied hard and graduated at the top of his class in law school when he was nineteen. Armed with this victory, Mihir decided to do something extraordinary—to study law in England, even though he was penniless!

After months of trying, he convinced the Odisha state government to help him. Finally, with a one-way ticket and £10 in his pocket, Mihir was on his way to London. Soon, he realized he didn't have enough money to live in the UK, let alone attend law classes. So, he did several odd jobs and completed his education by learning law from library books.

It was the year after India's Independence. Mihir decided to make his young nation proud by swimming across the English Channel—one of the toughest swims in the world. But Mihir had no training. So, he began swimming practice while learning about the conditions and the creatures of the Channel. His first attempt to swim across the strait failed, but he kept training for another three years. Finally, in 1958, covered in mustard oil to protect him from the cold, Mihir tried again. In fourteen hours and forty-five minutes, he had swum across the Channel, showing everyone the power of a dream!

Mihir went on to become the first man to swim the oceans of five continents in one year! From swimming with poisonous jellyfish to being chased by sharks in cold waters, Mihir proved to the world that Indians were no longer afraid.

PADMA
SHRI
1959

MILKHA SINGH

FLYING SIKH

1929–2021

The Partition of British India into India and Pakistan was a turbulent period. There was terrible violence on both sides of the border. At the time, Milkha Singh and his family were living in Pakistan. One day, when a mob of people attacked their village, Milkha's father told him to run away. 'Bhaag Milkha, bhaag,' his father shouted, asking Milkha to run for his life. Little did Milkha know that running would become his future.

Milkha escaped to India and tried to build a life in Delhi. He joined the Indian army, where he was introduced to running. He took to the sport and eventually became an athlete. After years of training, Milkha was ready to participate in a big race—the Commonwealth Games in London! People had high hopes for him, but Milkha was nervous. The night before the race, he had nightmares about all that could go wrong. *Should I just quit?* he wondered.

In the race, Milkha was pitted against some of the world's finest athletes. Milkha stood at the starting line with 'INDIA' written across his T-shirt. His heart was pounding; he was determined to make his country proud. Milkha's legs moved like lightning. He sprinted down the track as wild cries of 'Come on, Singh!' echoed all around. Flying across the track, he crossed the finish line in the first place. India had won her first gold medal in the Commonwealth Games!

Milkha's victory at the Commonwealth Games brought the whole country together. When asked what he wanted as a reward, Milkha requested the then prime minister, Jawaharlal Nehru, to declare a national holiday. After all, what brings a nation more joy than an unexpected holiday!

NARTHAKI NATARAJ

- -

DOYENNE OF DANCE
1964–PRESENT

PADMA SHRI 2019

Narthaki was born in a hamlet near Madurai. When she was eleven years old, something awful happened to Narthaki—her family turned their backs on her. This was because Narthaki was a transgender girl. Though she was born as a boy, she thought of herself as a girl. Unfortunately, few people understood how Narthaki felt.

Narthaki's family turned her out, but she met someone who understood and supported her. Shakti was a transgender person like Narthaki, and they became best friends and companions. They spent their days playing in a temple compound, hanging from the sprawling branches of a majestic banyan tree. Narthaki dreamt of becoming a dancer but had no formal training. Even then, the two friends would practise their dance and gymnastics.

Eventually, Narthaki's dancing and dreaming paid off. She found a guru in Tanjore and started training in classical dance. She became a Bharatnatyam dancer and started performing all over the world. Narthaki made history when she became the first transgender person to join the State Development Policy Council of Tamil Nadu and win a Padma Shri.

Narthaki's achievements are ground-breaking, and she is a strong supporter of the transgender community. But she wants people to know her first and foremost as a dancer. Narthaki and her best friend Shakti have set up a school of dance that welcomes students from all walks of life, including transgenders.

For Narthaki, dance has become a magical way to heal the wounds that society has caused. Her friendship with Shakti gave her the courage to face challenges and become a dancer. Narthaki once said, 'We created a world for ourselves where we would happily play and dance; we have carried that world with us to this day.'

NEIDONUO ANGAMI

MOTHER OF PEACE
1950–PRESENT

n the magical land of Nagaland, where jungles whisper secrets and mountains stand tall, there lives a brave woman named Neidonuo. Growing up, she saw the pain of war and decided to change things for the better.

In 1947, a day before India declared independence, Nagaland declared itself independent. India did not recognize this, and years of fighting followed between the Indian government and the Naga people. As a child of war, Neidonuo spent her early life hiding in jungles to stay safe from the bullets that whizzed through the air. Her father, an interpreter with the government, was captured and lost his life tragically. The bullets weren't the only things that caused harm. All the fighting led many Naga people to become drug and alcohol addicts. Neidonuo's heart ached for her people.

When Neidonuo became a mother, she saw her children growing up in the same dangerous environment. She knew something had to be done. Together with other brave women, she formed the Naga Mothers' Association (NMA) to help mothers who, like her, were watching their children struggle. Neidonuo travelled across Nagaland, speaking out against the bloodshed and urging Naga leaders to end the violence.

Thousands of grieving mothers who had lost their children found a voice in Neidonuo's courageous words. With her head held high, Neidonuo stood for peace and even offered to conduct talks with the government.

Peace talks were dangerous because bullets could be fired at any point, but Neidonuo's bravery knew no bounds. In those meetings, where she played the role of a mediator, bridges were built, and trust blossomed between the warring sides. Slowly, the fighting began to subside, and a new era of hope started in Nagaland.

Growing up, Neidonuo had never known a peaceful life. Yet she is known as the 'mother of peace', reminding the world that even in the darkest of times, the strength of a mother's love can heal wounds.

PANDIT JASRAJ

MODERN TANSEN

1930-2020

Born into a family of musicians, Jasraj was surrounded by music from his very first breath. When he was about four years old, Jasraj's father was chosen to be a musician in a royal court. However, destiny took an unforeseen turn. Unfortunately, his father passed away on the very day he was to join the court. Sadness descended upon what should have been a happy day.

In spite of this loss, Jasraj pursued music. Once he was older, he travelled to Gujarat to learn music and began his career as a tabla artist. But Jasraj realized what he really wanted to do was sing! At twenty-two, he performed for the king of Nepal, who was so impressed that he awarded Jasraj 5,000 gold coins. Jasraj nearly fainted!

Music became Jasraj's passion, and he practised it fourteen hours a day. Not only was Jasraj's signing making waves in India, but it was also taking over stages all over the world!

Once, at a sunrise concert in Varanasi, Jasraj was performing Raga Todi in front of a huge crowd. Suddenly, without warning, a deer ran on to the stage. It was an extraordinary moment. It is said that in the sixteenth century, the famous musician Tansen drew a herd of deer from the forest while singing the same raga! Like the legendary Tansen, Jasraj, too, could compel the creatures of the universe with the beauty of his voice. Another time, when Jasraj was singing Raga Malhar, which is associated with rainfall, it started to rain out of nowhere! 'If you sing from within, you attract the universe . . . I won't say I was responsible for that, but my music was responsible,' said Jasraj.

Jasraj did not believe in limiting classical music to experts. Up until his final days, he was conducting classes on Skype. He said that music should be heard by everyone, including deer!

PANDIT RAVI SHANKAR

GODFATHER OF WORLD MUSIC

1920–2012

When Ravi was a child, his brother left India to work in Paris. After some time, Ravi joined his brother in Paris and was exposed to music and dance from all over the world. Even though Ravi returned to India to learn the sitar, the sowed during his travel abroad had taken root—he would forever experiment with global music.

Ravi spent his life performing alongside some of the greatest musicians in the world. In fact, George Harrison, the guitarist of The Beatles—the most popular band in the world—wanted Ravi to teach him the sitar. George came to India to learn from Ravi and even wore a disguise so that he would not be recognized by his fans! To escape the crowds, Ravi and George went to peaceful Kashmir. On a houseboat by the shimmering lake waters, Ravi taught George the sitar. They practised from sunrise to sunset, filling the air with beautiful melodies.

It wasn't just the sitar that Ravi taught George. Once, George stepped over the sitar when he went to answer the phone. Ravi promptly slapped George on the leg for not showing enough respect for the instrument. He told George that in Indian culture, respect given to musical instruments was equal to that given to God. It was a lesson that George never forgot.

Ravi went on to do many incredible things, including organizing one of the first rock concerts for charity in New York. Great musicians such as Eric Clapton and Bob Dylan performed at the concert. Through it all, Ravi never stopped experimenting. 'The beauty of our music is the ability to improvise endlessly,' he once said, 'and that is my forte—I never know what I am going to do in the next two seconds, and that is still a great thrill.'

PADMA
SHRI
1990

PADMA
BHUSHAN
2002

PADMA
VIBHUSHAN
2022

PRABHA ATRE

SUNRISE OF MUSIC

1932–2024

Prabha, who has received all three Padma awards for music, did not come from a family of musicians. When Prabha was eight, her mother became ill, and that's when Prabha's father had an idea. He thought that harmonium lessons might help Prabha's mother recover. After all, music is said to have healing powers. The lessons began, but Prabha's mother did not find them exciting and quit after a few classes. But guess who developed an interest? Little Prabha! In those few lessons, Prabha was captivated! And from that moment on, music became Prabha's passion.

Prabha began her education in music under renowned gurus of classical music. Later, she even earned a doctorate in music. Prabha wanted Hindustani classical music to be appreciated all over the world. 'Music has to go beyond technique . . .' she said. '. . . It should sing through time and place.' And so she travelled the globe, becoming the first female Indian artist to give full-length concerts in the West.

To make sure that the next generation also appreciated classical music, she taught thousands of students. Prabha was perhaps one of the few musicians who was a full-time teacher and a top-class performer at the same time. It is no wonder that many call her 'Gaan Prabha', the sunrise of music.

Once, a thief broke into her home and stole some valuables. It was 4:30 a.m., and Prabha was practising her music. The sunrise of music was singing at sunrise. Later, she told the police that even though she had heard the noises, she continued singing! Nothing could come in the way of her music practice. 'I want to sing until my last breath,' Prabha would say. What a stroke of luck that her father arranged music lessons for Prabha's mother all those years ago.

RUSKIN BOND

MASTER STORYTELLER
1934-PRESENT

Open any Ruskin Bond book, and you will instantly be transported to a magical world! The joy of kind people, the warmth of a family dinner and long walks in misty mountains comfort the reader. Maybe Ruskin writes about these joys because his childhood was not as happy. Ruskin's parents separated when he was very young, and by the time he was ten, his father had passed away. Books became his best friends during this difficult time.

As a young man, Ruskin wanted to be a writer, but there weren't many publishers in India who were bringing out books in English. Ruskin left for England, and there he published his first novel, which went on to win a big prize! Still, there was a problem. Even though his parents were British, Ruskin found that England didn't inspire him. Without motivation, he found it difficult to write. Ruskin missed India terribly, and so he made a life-changing decision. He packed his bags and sailed back to his beloved India!

At first, things were tough when he returned. Books in English were still not being published as much. Ruskin wrote newspaper columns to earn some money. At times, he even took on odd jobs. Still, he kept writing his own stories. When English publishers finally came to India, Ruskin had a treasure trove of his stories ready to be shown to them!

Ruskin has a secret to his magical storytelling—he is interested in the small things. Once, the writer spent a long time watching a snail cross a road. 'There were a lot of cars, and even trucks speeding up and down the road. But the snail did manage to get across!' said Ruskin. Soon after, he published a poem titled *The Snail*. The master of words proved that life can never be boring, unless you *make* it boring.

SAINA NEHWAL

SPORTS STAR
1990–PRESENT

PADMA SHRI 2010

PADMA BHUSHAN 2016

One could say that badminton was in Saina's genes. Growing up in Haryana, little Saina would watch her mother whiz across the badminton court and dream of following in her footsteps. Her mother was a state-level badminton player, but Saina wanted to go further.

When she was eight years old, Saina moved to Hyderabad with her family. In a new place, surrounded by people who spoke a language she didn't understand, Saina spent most of her time watching her parents play badminton. Eventually, she picked up the racket and started playing, too. Soon, her talent was spotted by a coach, and he signed her up for formal classes. Sania dreamed of reaching the nationals and making her mother proud! She practised hard, and within a year, Saina had taken the badminton court by storm. It was like she had a turbo engine in her shoes!

By 2006, Saina had conquered the Asian Satellite Badminton Tournament in India, not once but twice! She was like a superhero with a racket, breaking all records possible. At twenty-two, Saina became the first Indian badminton player to win at the Olympics. Returning to India with her bronze medal, Saina seemed unstoppable. Soon after, she was at the world number one rank in badminton, the first Indian woman to ever hold that position.

Over the years, Saina has suffered several sports injuries while playing badminton. But she hasn't given up playing and is working on healing her injuries.

So far, Saina's twelve-year-long badminton career has earned her twenty-four international titles, eleven of which are Super Series titles! And you know what is still burning strong? Her amazing spirit that never lets her quit! When asked why she continues to strive, Saina has a ready answer: 'Because players like to play. When the body stops, I will stop.'

SAROJ RAJ CHOWDHURY

TIGER DAD
1924–1982

PADMA
SHRI
1983

In the magnificent forests of Odisha, there lived a remarkable man named Saroj. Not only was he a forest official but also a true friend of the animals. One day, something extraordinary happened that changed his life forever.

A tigress had brought her three cubs to the River Khairi for a drink. When the villagers tried to scare the animals away, two cubs fled with their mother. But one little cub, too weak to run, was left behind, unprotected and alone. Saroj immediately adopted the two-month-old cub and named her Khairi, after the river where she was found. Saroj and his wife welcomed the cub into their home, and Khairi became their foster daughter. They lovingly fed her mutton and milk powder, and the weak little cub soon grew strong. In Saroj's home, Khairi had many other animals to play with. A crocodile, a bear cub, a blind hyena and a clever mongoose— all of whom had found love under Saroj's roof. Together, they became an extraordinary family! Khairi was everyone's favourite. She even slept on Saroj's bed. Although Saroj tried to release Khairi into the forest several times, she always found her way back to his house. It was as if she knew Saroj was her true family. Their bond was truly unbreakable. When Khairi died, Saroj was heartbroken. Not long after, he had a heart attack and passed away, too. It was as though his heart had beat for Khairi.

Saroj is often considered the father of wildlife education in India. He developed the pugmark tracking technique which is still used to count tigers in India's forests. He also helped launch the famous Project Tiger initiative. Whenever Saroj would meet other wildlife experts, his advice would always be the same: 'spend more time in the jungle rather than in comfortable offices because the forest is the greatest teacher of all'.

SATYAJIT RAY

- - - - - - - - - - -

CINEMA CZAR

1921–1992

PADMA SHRI 1958

PADMA BHUSHAN 1965

PADMA VIBHUSHAN 1976

Satyajit Ray is considered one of the best film-makers of all time. When he started making his first movie, *Pather Panchali*, he didn't know the first thing about film-making! But what Satyajit had was an idea.

To make a movie, you need cameramen, actors, musicians and many more skilled people. So, Satyajit gathered a group of technicians. Somehow, he even convinced the famous musician, Pandit Ravi Shankar, to compose the music of the film. Instead of picking famous actors, Satyajit chose ordinary people to act in the movie. He thought that regular people would make the story more real and heart-warming. And he turned out to be right!

There were other challenges, though. Satyajit had very little money, so he borrowed some and even took a loan. He did not want to compromise on anything. When people suggested he fake the rain in the movie, he insisted on shooting in the monsoon. During the filming, things often went wrong. Once, cows ate the flowers needed for an important scene. Satyajit waited patiently until the flowers bloomed again to shoot the scene. He wanted those flowers and nothing else! He knew that wonderful things were worth waiting for.

When the film's shooting was completed, MOMA, which is a famous art museum in New York, wanted to show it. Satyajit worked day and night to meet their deadline. *Pather Panchali* went on to become the first film in independent India to receive so much international recognition. After that, Satyajit didn't stop. He created more films that beautifully portrayed the lives of the main characters. Satyajit's movies weren't just movies; they were like treasure chests filled with stories that would live forever!

PADMA
VIBHUSHAN
1954

S.N. BOSE

PHENOMENAL PHYSICIST
1894–1974

Growing up, Satyendra Nath Bose was fascinated by logic and mathematics. His father, an accountant in the Indian Railways, would leave his son with a maths problem every day before going to work. This sharpened his skill for numbers. It was only natural that Bose would eventually become a great scholar of mathematics and physics, and a professor to boot!

Bose had an unusual claim to fame. He wrote a strikingly original paper on a concept in physics called Planck's Law. But no journal was willing to publish the paper. Without feeling dejected, Bose took a bold step. He sent the paper straight to Albert Einstein—one of the greatest physicists of all time—in Germany! Einstein instantly recognized Bose's genius and saw that this research was an important step forward in the field of physics. Einstein translated the paper into German and sent it for publication to a leading European journal.

This changed everything for Bose. From being a relatively unknown scholar in Bengal, he became an internationally recognized name in the field of science! He travelled to Europe to meet Einstein and other scientists, like Marie Curie. After two years, he returned to the University of Dacca (now Dhaka) and joined the Physics Department as a professor, eventually becoming its head.

What we know today as 'Bose Statistics', named after Bose, plays an important role in mathematics. A branch of Physics studies the different types of particles that form all objects and things on earth. A group of particles were named 'bosons' in Bose's honour. Einstein developed Bose's concept even further, and this theory came to be known as the Bose-Einstein condensate. Bose proved two clichés in one go: taking chances can pay off, and you should meet your heroes!

SUDHA MURTY

FIRST OF HER KIND
1950-PRESENT

India in the 1960s was very different from what the country is today. Back then, many families believed that girls shouldn't study subjects such as engineering. Unfortunately, Sudha's family was one of them. But Sudha's dream was to be an engineer. She was fascinated by how science could be applied in real life! When Sudha announced her dream to her family, it was as if she had dropped a bomb in the house.

Sudha's grandmother expressed her disappointment, saying that no man would marry a girl who was an engineer. Even her aunts said the same, and Sudha's grandfather advised her to study history instead. Her mother suggested a career in mathematics, while her father recommended medicine. But Sudha's resolve did not waver. Inspired by the fearless Chinese traveller and scholar, Hiuen Tsang, who followed his dreams, Sudha declared, 'I want to do engineering; come what may!'

Finally, after convincing her family, Sudha enrolled in her town's engineering college. But bigger challenges remained. Sudha was the only female student in the entire college! Again, her family tried to discourage her, but Sudha refused to change her field of study. College life was often difficult. Her male classmates didn't know how to react to a female student studying among them. She was as interesting as an alien to them. They would often play pranks on her and, sometimes, even pass hurtful comments. The college didn't even have a ladies' toilet! But Sudha focused on her studies and persevered. Eventually, and to the surprise of many, Sudha stood first in the university!

Today, Sudha is a beloved author and philanthropist. Even after all the success, Sudha never forgot the struggle of not having access to a toilet during her college day. She has gone on to build over 13,000 toilets in Karnataka alone.

TEEJAN BAI

POWERHOUSE PERFORMER
1956-PRESENT

When Teejan Bai grew up in a village in Chhattisgarh, things were quite different from how they are today. Girls were expected to get married when they were still children. Teejan was married off at the age of twelve. But soon, her life took a very unexpected turn.

Teejan was enamoured by the Pandavani, which is a traditional art form where people sing and dance to bring stories from the Mahabharata to life. The Pandavani is usually performed by men, and Teejan's family didn't want her to be singing and dancing. So, Teejan asking to perform the Pandavani was like asking for the moon— it was impossible! Teejan's family forbade her from performing, and those were some of the darkest days of her life. Still, the young girl didn't let those struggles stop her. She knew she was born to sing.

At thirteen, she bravely performed the Pandavani for the first time in another village. People loved her powerful voice and the way she told the story with music and rhythm. Even though her family and some others were still against her, Teejan stayed strong. Then, something truly incredible happened! A theatre director took notice of her talent. He saw the spark in her eyes, heard the magic in her voice and realized that her talent needed to be shared with the rest of the world.

After that, there was no looking back for Teejan. Her life became a grand adventure! She began performing in foreign countries, such as England and Germany, and also taught people about the beautiful Pandavani.

There was a time when Teejan was barred from performing the Pandavani. But today, she is the most famous Pandavani artist in the world, showing us the power of dancing to our own tune!

USHA CHAUMAR

COURAGEOUS CHANGEMAKER
1978–PRESENT

Even at the tender age of seven, Usha was doing a job. But it wasn't a job one might dream of having at any age. Usha was a manual scavenger, which meant she cleaned human waste, especially from toilets and open drains, with her bare hands. It was a difficult and dangerous job, and little Usha longed for a way out of this messy situation.

Usha continued doing this work even as a grown up. She had almost given up hope when she met Dr Pathak, the founder of Sulabh International. Dr Pathak had a brilliant idea. He suggested that Usha and others like her try different ways of earning a living, like tailoring or selling vegetables. Usha and her friends couldn't help but laugh at this idea. They wondered, 'Who would buy clothes from us? Who would eat our vegetables?' Some people thought these brave manual scavengers were dirty or 'untouchable'. These people wouldn't touch the things that manual scavengers like Usha touched. It was like having invisible walls around her. Besides, Usha was terrified to try something new. But then, Usha remembered that she had always wanted a better life. So, she dared to take a tiny step forward and said, 'Yes, I'll give it a try!' And those words unlocked a door to a whole new world!

Usha learned to read and write. She convinced her friends and even her mother-in-law to leave behind their scavenging tools and join her on this exciting new journey. The village began to change. New toilets popped up. Usha's old job was no longer needed, and her village turned into a cleaner, happier place. And leading this transformation, like a captain steering a ship through stormy seas, was none other than Usha!

Today, Usha leads Sulabh. She travels the world, talking about her journey from cleaning toilets to cleaning up the world from something even bigger, which is injustice.

USTAD BADE GHULAM ALI KHAN

MASTER OF BREATH

1902–1968

PADMA
BHUSHAN
1962

In a home overflowing with the wonders of music, a young boy named Ghulam lived with his family. His father and his uncles were gifted musicians who filled their home with enchanting tunes. Sadly, Ghulam lost his father and uncles when he was still young. With them gone, the house grew silent, and Ghulam's musical future became uncertain. That's when he decided to take matters into his own hands.

Ghulam searched for a place where he could be alone with his music and found a deserted monument near the River Ravi in Pakistan. Under the open sky, he would rehearse all night determinedly. At first, Ghulam would be all alone during these practice sessions, with only the stars as his audience. But as word of his talent spread, a curious crowd began to gather. His 'concerts' had no expensive tickets or huge auditoriums. They took place right there, by the river, with tradesmen and travellers as his spellbound listeners. This nightly *riyaz* gave Ghulam the stamina to sing for hours on end. It was under the night sky that he learned the music of nature—the chirping crickets, the rustling wind—and let it shape his melodies.

Over time, Ghulam's fame soared, and he came to be known as Ustad Bade Ghulam Ali. People hailed him as the Tansen of the twentieth century. When Bade Ghulam's life journey was nearing its end, his students asked how they could honour him. Can you imagine what he asked for? Perhaps a grand monument with his name on it? No! Bade Ghulam asked his students to raise funds to help other musicians. The man who began his career singing by a monument didn't want a monument dedicated to him. And that's how Bade Ghulam's name continues to shine—not in stone, but in the music he left behind.

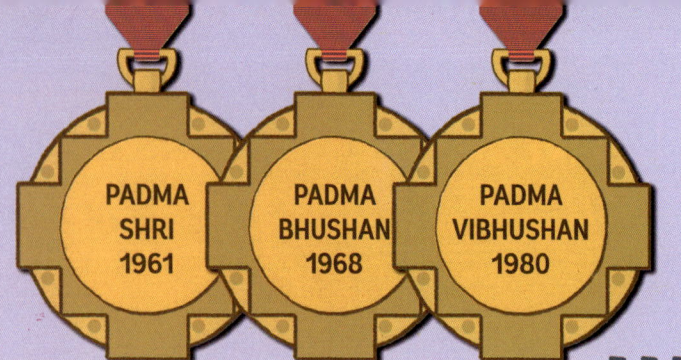

PADMA
SHRI
1961

PADMA
BHUSHAN
1968

PADMA
VIBHUSHAN
1980

USTAD BISMILLAH KHAN

MAESTRO OF BENARES
1916–2006

When Qamruddin Khan was born, his grandfather was so delighted that he exclaimed, 'Bismillah!' which means in the name of Allah. So, everyone called the baby Bismillah. Little did the boy know that this special name would bring so much luck into his life.

When Bismillah was around six, he moved to Benares (now Varanasi), where he watched his uncle playing the *shehnai* in the temples. Inspired, he began learning to play the wind instrument under his uncle's guidance. Soon, he became a skilled player. Many people did not consider the shehnai as a proper art form at that time, but Bismillah's playing left everyone who was listening in awe.

On 15 August 1947, the day of India's independence, Bismillah was asked to play the shehnai on national radio to celebrate the nation's freedom. It was a great honour for him. Then, in 1965, the artist gave his first international performance at the Edinburgh Festival. People from all over the world had gathered to listen, and when they heard the maestro, they were spellbound! Thereafter, he recorded several albums and travelled all over the world, giving concerts. Through it all, Bismillah led a simple life free from luxury.

Bismillah's love for Benares was legendary. He insisted he would never leave the city. If anyone wanted to see him, even a maharaja, they would have to come to Benares! Once, a wealthy gentleman asked Bismillah to move to the United States, promising to pay for everything if only Bismillah agreed. But the musician said, 'First, make me a Benares in America.' Needless to say, Bismillah stayed back in Benares, and it was there, by the holy river Ganga, that he breathed his last.

PADMA
SHRI
1983

VIJAY AMRITRAJ

TRUE CHAMPION
1953–PRESENT

Meet two brothers, Anand and Vijay. As children, Anand was a strong boy, whereas Vijay was weak and asthmatic. This made it difficult for him to play sports. But his parents encouraged him to play tennis with his brother, hoping it would make him healthier. Slowly and steadily, Vijay began to feel stronger, and his game improved. However, there was a problem—tennis training required money, and their family was struggling to manage their budget. That's when Vijay's mother, Margaret, came to the rescue. She started a business selling cardboard boxes for extra income.

Thanks to his family's support, Vijay excelled in tennis. In 1974, both Vijay and Anand reached the finals of the Davis Cup in South Africa—a very exciting moment for the whole country. If India won the Cup, it would be a major sporting first. It was the chance of a lifetime, and both brothers were excited to bring home the trophy. But there was an issue. At that time, South Africa was practicing apartheid, a terrible system that treated people unfairly based on their skin colour. The Indian government wanted the players to stand up against apartheid and boycott the match. Vijay was in a dilemma—should he play in the Davis Cup or not? He chose what he believed was right and boycotted the tournament. He said, 'As an athlete, I wanted to win the Davis Cup . . . but boycotting the Cup was the best thing we did. It was for what the world believed in and what we believed in.'

Vijay continued to speak against apartheid and was appointed as a UN Messenger of Peace. For an incredible fourteen years, Vijay was ranked as the number one tennis player in Asia. Vijay's name means 'victory' and he proved to be a true winner—in sports and in life!

VISWANATHAN ANAND

In the realm of chess, no one has made a mark quite like Viswanathan Anand. From the age of six, Anand began to learn the secrets of chess from his mother. She came from a family of chess lovers, and taught her son everything she knew about the game.

When Anand was around eight, the family moved to Manila, where chess was gaining popularity. There, he grew interested in a local television chess programme. The trouble was that the show was telecast during the day, the hours when Anand was in school. This was back in the day when you couldn't watch TV programmes whenever you wanted. So, every day, Anand's mom would watch the TV show and make notes about the different chess moves.

Each episode on the show ended with a chess contest, and viewers were asked to send in their answers. The prize was a free book. Every day, when Anand returned from school, he would go over the contest question with his mother and send his answer to the TV station. Anand was winning so many contests that the station had to call and beg him to stop sending entries. Instead, they invited him to their library and said he could read any book there. With Anand contesting, no one else was getting a chance to win!

Anand became popular in the world of international chess in the 1980s. Soon, everyone started calling Anand the 'Lightning Kid' because he made his chess moves as fast as lightning. Anand went on to become India's first Chess Grandmaster and won the World Chess Championship five times. He was the first sportsperson to be awarded the Padma Vibhushan. The Lightning Kid won the Padma Shri at the age of nineteen, becoming the youngest person ever to win it.

ACKNOWLEDGEMENTS

I've been lucky to work with an excellent team at Penguin Random House India. Sohini Mitra, who believed in this book without hesitation. Sushmita Chatterjee, editor extraordinaire, who championed this book and brought it to life with both her talent and her enthusiasm. Shabari Choudhury, who weeded out errors with a fine-toothed comb. A special thanks to Samar Bansal for his ideas on design and layout. And, of course, David Yambem, whose superb illustrations brought *The Padmas* to life.

I was blessed to find an incredible resource in Lakshmi Mitra, who made the research process so much easier. I can't imagine doing this book without you.

In some ways, this book is a labour of love for my parents, Pinku and Pradeep Jhalani. They created a home free of prejudice where all that mattered was love for the country, a simple philosophy that has become both rare and precious.

My children, Zoya and Jahan, who haven't had the privilege of living in India. The longer they live away from home, the more I want to tell them the stories.

NEHA J HIRANANDANI

is an author and columnist whose columns have appeared in *The Indian Express*, Huffington Post, NDTV and *Vogue*, among others. She holds degrees in literature and education from Wellesley College and Harvard University. Her first book, *Girl Power!*, was a national bestseller, and she recently launched her second book, *iParent*, about living in the digital age.

DAVID YAMBEM

is an animator and illustrator from Kakching, a town in Manipur. He loves cooking and experimenting with food. He is passionate about photography and is a plant and wildlife enthusiast.

Scan QR code to access the
Penguin Random House India website